GRAINS AMONG THE CHAFF

GRAINS AMONG THE CHAFF

Jay Appleton

illustrated by
Geoffrey Shovelton

The Wildhern Press 2008

Jay Appleton is an Emeritus Professor of Geography at the University of Hull. His publictions include The Poetry of Habitat, The Experience of Landscape and a collection of poems, The Cottingham Collection

Geoffry Shovelton began humorous drawing while at school. He found many subjects for humour in the opera companies for which he sang. He was Principal Tenor for the D'Oyly Carte Opera Company from 1975 to 1982, many drawings inspired by Gilbert and Sullivan featured in the Palace Peeper, the magazine of the New York G&S Society.

Published by

The Wildhern press

131 High St.
Teddington
Middlesex TW11 8HH

ISBN 978-1-84830-074-3

GRAINS AMONG THE CHAFF

CONTENTS

IV MUSIC

V. SPORT

VI. FOOD

Introducing Us

The writer is an elderly
Professor of Geography.
Like every academic type
He earned his living talking tripe,
Which is a mortifying state
For anyone to contemplate;
So who can blame him if he tries
To show a little enterprise
Whiling away the idle hour,
Secluded in his ivory tower,
Composing little bits of verse?
Be thankful that it's nothing worse.

His partner in this deed of crime
For some considerable time
Has earned an honest crust or two
By singing *Faust* and *Nanki-Poo*,
With many other roles as well,
And not too badly, truth to tell.
But still he also finds it nice
To cultivate a secret vice,
And now and then, before he sings,
He'll snatch a moment in the wings
And fix on some unwitting wretch
To be the subject of a sketch.

This little venture thus combines
Our two respective leisure-lines,
And we have jointly had recourse
To jumping on one hobby-horse.

"Oh, winnow all my folly, folly, folly and you'll find
There's a grain or two of truth among the chaff!"

Jack Point in *The Yeoman of the Guard*

1 LIT. AND PHIL.

Theory Versus Practice

The Captain of Artillery
  Was quite a clever chap;
He taught ballistic theory
  And how to read a map.
The lure of guns and gunnery
  He never could resist,
But on the range his battery
  Invariably missed.

Consider, on the contrary,
  The pigeon on the wing.
About ballistic theory
  He didn't know a thing;
But, when he dropped maliciously
  His load of you-know-what,
With never-erring certainty
  He proved a deadly shot.

I must admit in honesty
  The notion that this bird
Had plotted a trajectory
  Is patently absurd;
And yet incontrovertibly
  He spotted from the sky
The Captain of Artillery
  And hit him in the eye.

The logical corollary
  Of this my little rhyme
Is that ballistic theory
  Is just a waste of time.
The Captain of Artillery
  Soon wiped away the mess
And took up ornithology
  With rather more success!

Shakespeare For Today

I genuinely wish I knew
Why all producers take the view
That, if they do a Shakespeare play,
They must adapt it for today.
If their intention is to raise
The *timeless* message of the plays,
Which I can only understand
Under their patronising hand,
They give gratuitous offence,
Insulting my intelligence.
Though I am old and on the shelf,
I'd rather work it out myself.
And yet I wonder, if I tried
To set my prejudice aside,
Whether I, too, might come to see
Some virtue in this gimmickry.
Perhaps we only can express
Meaningful themes in modern dress.
Henry the Fourth (Parts One and Two)
Will serve to show what we could do;
Hal is a skinhead layabout;
Falstaff becomes a lager lout;
Hotspur, I guess, would not be slain
At Shrewsbury, but White Hart Lane.
Alternatively Henry Five
Assuredly would come alive
If Churchill tanks should blaze their way
Into the breach on Crispin's Day.
When the conspirators agree
To finish Caesar's tyranny,
Why use a dagger when one might
Have opted for an Armalite?
Prospero's musack-haunted isle
Reverberates with reggae, while

They've written out poor Caliban,
That culturally-challenged man,
Because he seems, in retrospect,
Politically incorrect.
Then why be spatially constrained
By venues which the Bard ordained?
The world's our oyster; we can use
Any location we may choose.
Othello probably was not
A *bona fide* Cypriot,
So why not relocate the play
In New Orleans or Monte Rey?
And Shylock, too, would not have been
Out of his depth in Golders Green.
Though Beatrice and Benedick
In Italy may bore you sick,
They might engender much ado
In Milton Keynes or Timbuktu.
The battlements of Elsinore
Have no real meaning any more,
And Hamlet might as well declare
His dark forebodings anywhere;
The question then, presumably,
Is *where* to be or not to be?

So let the tight-jeaned Romeo flirt
With Juliet in a miniskirt;
Let Lear be black and Hamlet gay;
Update the message for today.
Shakespeare be born again!   But wait!
If we're to bring him up to date,
There's one thing troubles me a bit -
The language simply doesn't fit.
Real people in the here-and-now
Don't speak in terms of 'thee' and 'thou',
Or use iambic prosody
Or pentametric pedantry.
New bottles, we are told, will do,
But only if the wine is new.
A man in period attire
Can get away with 'Prithee, sire',
But if he wears a Stetson hat
It makes him sound a proper prat.
So is this thespian liberty
Just as you like it?   No sirree!

The Generation Gap

However disconcerting be
The foibles of our progeny,
Which will not say or think or do
What we believed we'd taught it to,
It's more discouraging by far
To find what dolts its parents are.

Paradox

If any man is worth his salary,
A Lord Chief Justice's we should not grudge;
For how the hell can one contrive to be
Tight as a lord and sober as a judge?

Fashion

In this our day
    It is the fashion to enshrine
  In stark and trenchant line
  What we most closely touch,
    However much
Our inclinations pull some other way;
This is our period, and here we stay.

So we must write
    In fashionable shades of ink,
  And if the kitchen sink
  Must be our writing-desk,
    The picturesque,
Labelled 'Victorian', 'naive' and 'trite',
Can gurgle down the plug-hole out of sight.

This is no time
  For Gentle Jesus on the walls
 Of aspidistra'd halls,
 Major and minor keys,
   Sweet harmonies,
Or realistic art, or (heinous crime)
Writing in metre, or, worse still, in rhyme.

The pen, set free
  From sentimental ballyhoo,
 Can turn attention to
 Contemporary things
   Like kidnappings,
Pollution, global warming, HIV,
Junkies and homosexuality.

And if we find
  The burning issues of the day
 Don't carry us away,
 We must be satisfied
   To stand aside,
Rather than flirt with some outmoded kind
Of intellectual pastime.   Never mind!

But just in case
  The point had not occurred to you,
 It's worth enquiring who
 Could possibly foresee
   How quick we'd be,
Having cast off one horny carapace,
To grow a hornier bastard in its place!

Weatherman

Weatherman he stand with his back to the fire
As the rain get worse and the wind get higher;
The clouds they threaten with ice and snow
And the glass that drop to an all-time low.
'That'll be' say the weatherman 'a terrible night.
'That don't bother me, sir, 'cos I'm all right.
'There's a big fire roar up the chimney stack -
'I're got a cold front but a mighty warm back!'

An Essay on Truth

When Albert signalled his intent,
  One evening in November,
To seek a seat in Parliament,
His father gave encouragement,
  But warned him to remember
That any lax morality
Or failure of integrity
    Can soon bring shame
    To smear the name
Of an unwary Member.

'Now take that fellow Washington',
  He said, 'It wouldn't hurt you
'To model your behaviour on
'That undisputed paragon
  'Of probity and virtue.
'Try to discover all you can
'About that great American,
    'And don't forget
    'Never to let
'Your baser thoughts subvert you.'

The only story Albert knew
  About this politician
Told how he took his hatchet to
A tree, and having chopped it through,
  Came up with this admission:
'Father, I cannot tell a lie;
'I have to say it was not I.
    'This noble tree
    'Amazingly
'Fell of its own volition!'

The little boy's temerity
  Earned Albert's admiration.
He vowed that retrospectively
He would redress this perjury
  And self-exoneration.
If *he* adhered to what was true,
This principle would see him through
    The knavish tricks
    Of politics,
  And spare his reputation.

'Twas in this mood of honesty
  He went electioneering.
The stupefied community
Greeted with incredulity
  The things that they were hearing.
When he described his party line
As full of things which sounded fine
    But in his view
    Were quite untrue
  They promptly started cheering.

A wave of popularity
  Secured him the election.
Constituents rejoiced to see
How soon their maverick M.P.
  Turned in this new direction.
The Party, on the other hand,
Utterly failed to understand
    His attitude,
    And deeply rued
  This streak of insurrection.

Right from his very first debate
  He never had his heart in
Conspiracies to denigrate
The Opposition's mental state,
  Nor would he take a part in

Urging *his* Party's policies,
Which he pronounced 'a pack of lies -
   'A specious lot
   'Of tommy rot,
 'My eye and Betty Martin!'

So Albert found himself one day
  Confronting the Committee.
'Such innocent naïveté,
'Which never would succeed', said they,
 'In commerce or the City,
'Was similarly never meant
'For the High Court of Parliament;
   'It is a view
   'More suited to
 'The world of Walter Mitty!'

'Albert', they said, 'What will you do?
  'Remain a politician,
'Or follow your commitment to
'Proclaiming only what is true
  'And seek some other mission?'
Said he 'However hard I try,
'I cannot bring myself to lie',
   So off he went
   To Parliament
  To ponder his position.

Misgivings entered Albert's head
  Too numerous to mention.
What if he'd misinterpreted
What devious little George had said,
  Mistaking his intention?
So off he went to buy an axe
And join a team of lumberjacks
   Whose expertise
   In felling trees
  Had come to his attention.

He soon acquired dexterity
  With stamina to match it,
And when the opportunity
Arose to fell another tree
  He would be quick to snatch it.
Valiant-for-Truth, he stood his ground,
And every time a tree was downed
    He'd say "'Twas I,
    'I cannot lie,
  'I did it with my hatchet.'

Albert, so rumour says, has gone,
  Fired with his new vocation,
Grimly resolved to practise on
The forests of the Amazon
  His work of devastation.
Those who respect veracity
Had better stick to forestry;
    If truth should mix
    With politics -
  That *would* be a sensation!

II The Church

The Church of England PLC

Dearly beloved brethren, let us pray
That modern management has come to stay.

The Church of England plc
Is heading for prosperity,
Its indigence of yesterday
Now resolutely swept away.
Improved efficiency became
The stated object of the game.
Sound fiscal policies with tight
Administrative oversight
Must now endeavour to repair
The legacy of *laissez-faire*
By inexperienced amateurs
Which blighted those mismanaged years.
The new regime is now in place;
Reforming measures gather pace;
New management techniques abound
To turn the ailing business round.
Assessment exercises too
Measure the work the clergy do;
Ex-army officers create
A brand new Church Inspectorate
Threatening parsons every day
With work-related merit pay.
Market researchers scan the pews
For evidence of under-use;
League tables tell their dismal tale,
Highlighting parishes which fail.
Each parish church in future must
Be managed by a separate Trust
Unless it first decides to be
An independent company.

The Stock Exchange is listing these
Under 'Divine Utilities';
(I note that Holy Trinity
Is up a point at ninety-three,
Whereas St Peter & St Paul
Has registered a modest fall).
To bishops now we have to give
The title 'Chief Executive'
And watch their stipends overnight
Go escalating out of sight,
Paid for by mass redundancies
In each cost-cutting diocese.
Archdeacons now are whisked away
To study for the MBA,
While rural deans are likewise sent
To learn financial management.
Internal markets guarantee
High levels of efficiency.
Ofpray, the Regulator, says
How much the congregation pays;
So much for this, so much for that,
Ten quid for a Magnificat,
Five for an anthem or a hymn,
Each at the Regulator's whim!
And any church which overspends
Has somehow got to make amends.
It's not unusual to see
A notice-board with this decree:
'No funerals conducted here
'Until the next financial year;
'(Fundholding clergy may apply
'For leave to bury those who die)'.
With sponsorship there now arise
All sorts of opportunities;
The cost of christenings will be
Met by the water company,
While every preacher tries to make
Room for a short commercial break.

Banners proceeding down the aisle
Carry commercial logos, while
Richly embroidered copes proclaim
In gleaming gold a sponsor's name.
Our vicar's text on Easter Day
Was 'Market forces rule, O.K.?',
And when he's visiting the sick
He watches the arithmetic;
The patient, venue, time and date
Are written down in triplicate;
Accountants settle which amount
Is debited to which account.
The flow of paper, so I'm told
Has multiplied an hundredfold,
Which takes the clergyman so long
He's had to cancel Evensong.
They forecast Mattins will be next
Unless he finds another text.
Nevertheless we all agree
The Church of England plc
Has left its penury behind -
Triumph of matter over mind!
The fiscal future's looking bright.
I just hope God's a Thatcherite!

Trinitarianism

Though matters of doctrine may keep them apart,
The preachers are all Trinitarians at heart;
They just can't resist it when things come in threes;
They fall for the triplet like mice for the cheese.
So bell, book and candle, the tools of the priest,
Are used for erasing the Mark of the Beast,
For nourishing virtue and probity, while
Demolishing Mephistophelian guile;
And hook, line and sinker, the fisherman's friends,
May equally serve theological ends;
The hooks catch the sinners, the line pulls them in,
The sinker enforces the wages of sin.
Though lock, stock and barrel are parts of a gun,
The saying is just a rhetorical one;
The theme of commitment this cliché implies
Is grist to the mill in a clergyman's eyes;
He'll bundle it into a Sunday address;
For its literal meaning he couldn't care less.
The World and the Devil would never suffice;
'The Flesh' adds the rhythm as well as the spice.
Each Tom, Dick and Harry must lay down his load
When he gets to the end of life's troublesome road;
A chorus of angels acclaims them on high
As left, right and centre they head for the sky.
The bishop, the priest and the deacon as well -
They may go to Heaven, they may go to Hell;
But one thing is sure, like I said at the start,
The preachers are all Trinitarians at heart.

Snake in the Grass
or Satan Strikes Again*

Out of the bowels of the earth
I slither from my lowly lair,
Scheming away for all I'm worth
To cause confusion and despair.

Adam and Eve have passed away,
And Eden's apple orchard too,
But here in England every day
There's diabolic work to do.

To further my satanic plan
I slither through the countryside,
Creating havoc where I can
And spreading chaos far and wide.

If anything should bar my way
I slither sinuously round,
And, if that doesn't work, I may
Discreetly slither underground.

The disillusioned men of Kent,
Grimly resolved to banish me,
Express their disillusionment
With bitter animosity.

They come at me with might and main,
They come at me with sticks and staves,
Frantic to drive me back again,
Like King Canute before the waves.

The brigadiers of Tunbridge Wells
Write to *The Times* in vitriol;

They curse me with malignant spells
And drown their grief in alcohol.

Dyspeptic colonels mourn the loss
Of peace, of quiet, of repose;
Sinister threats make Charing cross
And politicians come to blows.

Demented squires in impotence
Through woods and meadows watch me slink,
Confederated in defence
Against the Channel Tunnel Link.

What if the colonels blow a fuse!
What if the brigadiers explode!
They go to meet their Waterloos;
I'm heading for the Euston Road!

* reprinted from *Landscape Research Extra* with
permission

Male and Female Created He Them

Genesis: i: 27.

The Reverend Rita Farthingale
Regretted she was not a male.
If not a bishop, then at least
She wanted to become a priest,
And found it hard to understand
Why she was permanently banned.
Her friendly Bishop was a saint
And sympathised with her complaint,
But made it clear he couldn't do
What Canon Law forbade him to.
'To be a deacon, that's OK,
'But not a priest, I'm sad to say;
'The gender rule is paramount.
'You haven't got the bits that count!
'But maybe you could compensate,
'If you could clearly demonstrate
'*Symbols* of masculinity
'To counter your deficiency.
'If every female attribute
'Was catapulted down the chute,
'It's possible I'd take the view
'This was the best that you could do;
'And, though it might be far from wise,
'I might accept a compromise.'
Rita responded eagerly
To this ingenious strategy;
Though manifestly she must fail
As *biologically* male,
Behaviourally she might win
And purge the lamentable sin
Of never having been a man,
But just another also-ran.

25

The gentle, merciful and kind
She resolutely left behind;
So, when she met a little boy,
Distressed about a broken toy,
She ordered him to take a grip,
(No trembling of the upper lip!),
Strangling at birth the elements
Of weak, maternal sentiments.
The way was open now to hail
The ruthless, chauvinistic male.
The Reverend Rita thus began
To implement the Bishop's plan.
She took to spitting on the floor;
She wore her socks a month or more;
Washing-up dirty dishes, too,
She'd leave for someone else to do.
Tidiness she dismissed as bunk,
And filled her pockets up with junk.
Tobacco ash was everywhere,
With muddy footmarks here and there.
(She had three brothers, so she knew
What men habitually do).

Decorum vanished up the spout;
Four-letter words came tumbling out,
And every night the air was blue
With words she didn't think she knew.
She joined the fellows packing down
The lagers at The Rose and Crown;
She soon acquired a boozer's tum,
Nurtured a taste for chewing-gum,
Stuck pieces on the window-ledge
And urinated in the hedge.
And, though she never thought of these
As being *priestly* qualities,
She worked as hard as hard could be
To prove her masculinity.
She wore an artificial 'tache;

She even had the nerve to 'flash',
And when she found that didn't work,
She tried another manly quirk;
She went and got a bouncer's job,
And smacked intruders in the gob.
She practised rugby songs, and when
She used the door marked 'Gentlemen'
She confidently thought she must
Have merited the Bishop's trust.
'Surely', she said, these manly ways
'Are bound to earn the Bishop's praise,
'And qualify me at the least
'To be a manly parish priest!'

One day a formal letter came.
She saw it bore the Bishop's name.
'Dear Sister Farthingale', she read;
'The Synod's changed the rules' it said;
'So, if you still intend to be
'A priest, that's good enough for me.'
The Reverend Rita seized with glee
This golden opportunity,
And, celebrating with a gin,
She banged her application in.

Disturbing stories, it appears,
Had meanwhile reached the Bishop's ears,
And when one testimonial
Told how she'd engineered a brawl,
(Which Rita thought would surely be
A sign of her virility),
The Bishop was beset with doubt
And threw her application out.
But, like a charitable man,
He said 'I'll help you if I can,
'And see if I can find a job
'More suited to a common yob.'
This devastating punch below
The belt incensed the lady so,
That she reverted in a while
To something like her former style;
She quickly proved herself astute
Enough to find a shorter route,
And thus through female wiles acquired
The recognition she desired.
Now Rita has attained her goal,
And plays an influential role
In ordering the Church's life,
Having become a bishop's wife.

Intimations of Mortality from the Churchyard

I

Here lies the body of Father Bell;
His soul, alas, has gone to hell.
He strove to lead his flock to heaven.
Saved is the lump but lost the leaven.

II

Here lies the breadman, Albert Strutt,
Gone home to meet his Maker.
He was an ardent churchman but
A pretty lousy baker.

III

The prospect facing Doctor Flynn
Is not, alas, inviting.
Saint Peter would have let him in,
But couldn't read his writing.

29

Theological Speculations in a Harvest Field

There stood, erect and undulant,
  A fructose field of corn,
Whither a ruddy rabbit ran
  One ruddy August morn,

At which specific momentude
  From distant window-pane
The matutinal husbandman
  Surveyed the ripening grain.

The matutinal husbandman
  He ruminated thus:
'Yon animal's expectitude
  'Is catastrophicous!

'For when the bright condensicles
  'Before the sunbeams yield
'I'll send the ruddy combine in
  'And cut that ruddy field.

'Tis fifty-fifty certitude
  'Before I go to bed
'I'll have that ruddy rabbitoid
  'Discervicated, dead.

'I find some satisfactitude
  'That yonder animal
'Should be of my preparatives
  'Quite ignorantical!'

The Deitate, omnivident,
  Surveys this rustic scene
And cries 'This bumptious georgicant
  'Presumes to overween.

'When half the field be harvested
  'And half the field be not,
'I'll send a ruddy thunderstorm
  'And wreck the ruddy lot!'

The rabbit, that with ecstasy
  Embraced the splendent morn,
Now quakes in trepidivity
  Within the static corn.

The chattering mechanicon
  That flails the summer air
Injiculates the rabbitoid
  With palpitant despair.

But see! The vapours, cumuloid,
  Deponderate the sky,
And myriad microhydrocules
  Come cataclysing by.

The dessicated pedocult
  That bore the berried grain
Is made a spongy glutefact
  By saturific rain.

The sore-distempered husbandman,
  Furescent from the irk,
With muttered maledictitudes
  Relinquishes his work.

O gastrocentric rabbitoid,
  Perceive thy jeopardy.
The fascinating fructitude
  Renunciate and flee!

Umbrose beneath the crepuscule,
  The rabbit, fortified,
Essays to run the gaventlet
  Athwart the stubbletide.

Humilified the rabbitoid
  That thought to gust the corn!
Humilified the husbandman
  That gloated in the morn!

But what about the Deitate
  That sedulates on high?
That overweening hybricrat,
  Will none humilify?

The Deitate, convulsified
  In exultative fits,
Expires from ridibunditude,
  Humilified to bits!

III Love, Sex and Romance

From *Flirtation* p.44

Penelope and the Pulchritudinist

Penelope was known to be
A model of efficiency;
She kept her desk immaculate,
Her correspondence up to date,
No clutter in her pending tray
And all her files in good array;
And even when some malcontent
Accused her of mismanagement,
Although she knew that she was right,
She'd be unfailingly polite.
But though she had a lively brain,
She was indubitably plain,
And every day she wondered why
Romantic love had passed her by.
The men would regularly flirt
With every other bit of skirt,

(Behaving quite disgracefully),
But never with Penelope.
She phoned a pulchritudinist
Whose aid she purposed to enlist,
And after half an hour agreed
A programme to address her need.
For several days he worked apace
To reconstruct the lady's face,
And when he'd done re-modelling
He'd made her look quite ravishing.
Her cheeks were pastel-hued, and each
Wore the complexion of a peach;
With lips like rubies, teeth like pearls,
She out-performed the other girls.
Cascades of golden-gleaming hair
Hung in the jasmin-scented air,
And there she'd sit, from head to heel
Exuding lethal sex-appeal.
She thought it quite hilarious
To find herself voluptuous,
And when the fish began to bite
She shamelessly enjoyed the sight.
But what exactly lay in store
Was more than she had bargained for.
Instead of tempting Cupid's dart
And capturing some lonely heart,
She signalled quite the wrong intent
And soon had reason to repent.
The men among the office staff
Were always ready for a laugh,
And plaguing poor Penelope
They took all kinds of liberty.
From manager to office boy
They saw her as a cuddly toy.
One macho colleague, gingerly,
And with affected gallantry,
Began in his deceitful way
To test the water, so to say,

And in his most disarming style
He started with a friendly smile;
But when the smile became a leer
His shameful strategy was clear.
He pinched her bottom, stroked her hair,
And didn't look like stopping there;
So when the going got too tough
She said, 'That's it! I've had enough!',
'The pulchritudinist will know
'How to restore the status quo',
And in an hour or little more
He'd made her plainer than before.
He said, 'My dear Penelope,
'The only girls I ever see
'Are simply out to get their man
'By any strategy they can.
'Beauty in this beholder's eye
'Is not skin-deep, and that is why
'The thing that most impresses me
'Is overall efficiency;
'That sets a man like me alight;
'So what about a date tonight?'
The moral of this little verse
Is, 'When things go from bad to worse,
'Don't trust in the beautician's art;
'It's sure to land you in the cart.
'Leave it alone; it won't be missed -
'But watch the pulchritudinist!'

Lewd Limericks

I
There was an old boar who said 'How
'I fancy that elegant sow!'
  She responded 'All right,
  'Come and see me tonight',
To which he replied 'Why not now?'

II
A lovesick young budgerigah,
When asked by his anxious mama
  'What on earth do you get
  'From that flighty coquette?'
Inscrutably answered 'Aha!'

III
A lonely old ram I once knew
Said 'There's nothing whatever to do
  'But mess up the moor
  'With organic manure
'And dream of adorable ewe'

IV
Said the hind to her husband 'Tut tut!
'I believe you implicitly, but
  'Why is it, my deer,
  'At this time of the year
'You always get into a rut?'

V
'It's grossly unfair' said the snake,
'For one thing I'm thin as a rake.
  'For my love life', he hissed,
  'I just get in a twist;
'I'm nature's most dismal mistake!'

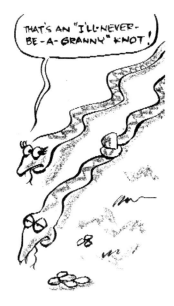

VI

'If you want to go mad' said the mole,
'You should try making love in a hole.
 'In my velveteen vest
 'I keep doing my best,
'But it isn't half taking its toll!'

VII

Said a grumpy old grayling called Greg
'Spare a thought for my problem, I beg;
 'In my marital life
 'There's no role for a wife;
'I just go to work on an egg.'

VIII

Two frogs were in heated debate
Discussing the best way to mate.
 'When you're up to your neck
 'In some perishing beck
'It's cold and it's wet - but it's great!'

IX
'Although I'm turned on' said the eel
'By your slimy and slithery feel,
'If you want me to flee
'To the Sargasso Sea,
'The idea doesn't really appeal.'

X
There once was a passionate spider,
Who said, as her mouth opened wider,
'I am hungry, my dove,
'And not only for love',
And the poor fellow finished inside 'er.

XI
An Australian breeder called Bruce
Said 'I grant you it's no bloody use,
'But by crossing a roo
'With a white cockatoo
'I've raised a marsupial goose!'

XII
When the owl makes a noise like a flute
He's telling his lover she's cute.
It may spell delight
To the bride of the night,
But to me it's a bit of a hoot!

XIII
Said the vet to the pregnant giraffe
'I know you're not wanting a calf,
'But the pill, don't you know,
'Had a long way to go,
'And it took it a week and a half.'

XIV
A whale who was feeling romantic
Trailed a submarine through the Atlantic.
  His short-lived elation
  Gave way to frustration,
Which drove the poor animal frantic.

XV
'Why on earth', said the maid to the rhino,
'Do you polish your horn on the lino?
  'Don't you think it's obscene?'
  He said 'What does that mean?'
She replied 'How the devil should I know?'

XVI
All manner of problems arise
When a hedgehog makes love; if he's wise,
  Renouncing temptation
  He'll shun copulation
Or risk an unwelcome surprise!

The Limitations of Love

Dearest Augusta, can it be
That, after all the bitter pain,
You condescend to turn to me,
The victim of your cold disdain?

In tortured visions I have seen
Your dimpled smile, and heard your laugh,
And now at last, my haughty queen,
You deign to send your photograph.

I would have granted any boon
The favour of one smile to earn,
And now you promise me the moon
And ask a trifle in return.

Have I not laid before your heart
Exotic herbs and fragrant flowers,
My pen, my muse, my humble art,
The lonely pain of lovesick hours?

And should you stoop to take it now,
You still should have my golden ring,
My every thought, my every vow,
My love, my life, my everything.

Still would my heart re-iterate
Each syllable I ever wrote . . .
But as the Tory Candidate
I'm damned if you shall have my vote!

Flirtation

(Spenserian Stanzas written in Bangkok Airport)

Can one conceive a less romantic place
For eyes to meet and secrets to be told,
Shelved and recessed with slots of hollowed space
And ochred slabs aspiring to be gold?
Guarded by gendarmes and by troops patrolled,
Courier-guided threads of human beads
Draw patterns in the random, uncontrolled
And multi-coloured mix of alien breeds,
Following where a uniformed official leads.

There was no magic moment to be prized,
No sudden act of finding you were there;
Rather a sense of having realised
We were already into an *affaire*.
First that warm waft of aromatic air,
More spiced than fragraant, then the tender touch
Progressing from the collar to the hair,
Stroking, entwining, grasping in its clutch.
No whispered words could tell a lover half as much.

As lords and ladies at a masquerade
Flirted with paramours they never knew,
So in the steaming afternoon we played,
Until I turned and thus disovered you,
Bright, burnished chestnut-brown, and nearly two.
Alas! That mountain of humanity
Seized you and rushed you to the ladies' loo,
Safe haven of impregnability
Against the madding crowd, the wicked world, and
me!

Mental Marriage

'Let me not to the marriage of true minds
'Admit impediments.'

W. Shakespeare - Sonnet 116.

The phrase 'the marriage of true minds'
Gives rise to doubts of many kinds.
The question that I find so odd is
Why just the minds and not the bodies,
Which most authorities would say
Have an important role to play?
Is 'mind' alone the reason why
People complete the nuptial tie?
How can one fit a wedding ring
On such an insubstantial thing?
Though thoughts and fancies have their place,
They're hardly easy to embrace,
And one would need to be a mug
To settle for a mental hug.
Erotic thoughts, however cute,
Can be at best a substitute,
And osculation can't enthral,
When merely psychological.
How can one kiss with tenderness
Given there are no lips to press?
How can one chuck one's lady fair
Under a chin that isn't there?
If it is just a mental state,
How can a couple consummate
A marriage in the legal sense?
It lies beyond their competence!
And then it cannot be denied
That marriage has its darker side.
What can the macho husband do

45

To beat his judy black and blue
Without a fist to black her eye?
(Not that she has one, by the by!).
When, bleary-eyed, he staggers in,
How can *she* wield the rolling-pin?
And what will happen when they find
Divorce is 'only in the mind'?
So not for me the common view
That Shakespeare knew a thing or two.
I'd say he didn't have a clue!

Research

Thesis

An amorous wench from Blantyre,
Who studied the way men perspire,
  Found an inverse relation
  Between perspiration
And distance from what they desire.

Abstract

The nearer you get,
The harder you sweat.

Turtle Dove My Foot!

Whoever chose the turtle dove
To symbolise romantic love?
A summer visitor, he's here
For rather less than half the year.
Does Cupid put his darts away
When nights are long and skies are grey?
Do not these very facts conspire
To further sexual desire?
'Turtle' is not the sort of name
To kindle a romantic flame;
The turtle's leather-textured face
Caricatures the human race.
This ugly quadruped, it's true,
Is wholly unrelated to
The Family *Columbidae*;
I've heard it said that probably
The appellation 'turtle' came
From '*turtur*', its Linnaean name,
An onomatopoeic word
Descriptive of a cooing bird.
The warbler, *Acrocephalus*,
Is every bit as amorous,
And with its sweet, romantic song
It pours its heart out all day long.
The cuckoo is a different case;
His reputation's a disgrace.
A fine advertisement he'd be
For marital fidelity!
But other species, truth to tell,
Would fit the image pretty well.
The nightingale was surely made
To charm us with her serenade;
Nightly she sings her song of love,

Unchallenged by the dormant dove.
Even the more ferocious fowls,
Like sparrow-hawks and eagle-owls,
Although aggressive, just the same
Find time to play the mating game.
Gannets returning to the nest
Display affection at its best;
By necking after every trip
They seal a loving partnership.
The love-bird ought to be a hit,
But somehow hasn't managed it.
Why should the sentimental dove
Claim this monopoly of love,
And exercise exclusive rights
To champion amorous delights?

Expose this over-rated bird
As sentimentally absurd!
Dislodge him from his pedestal!
He's just a pigeon, after all!

IV MUSIC

Orchestral Disharmony

Eye for eye, tooth for tooth   (Exodus xxi, 24)

The car park at the concert hall
  Was full to saturation,
And patrons of the festival
Were manifesting, one and all,
  The signs of irritation,
When there arrived a Cadillac,
Aristocratic, sleek and black,
    Whose occupant
    Was militant
  With ill-concealed frustration.

'The orchestra will have to wait',
  He said, 'Cos I'm the leader.'
(How he went on to fulminate
With all the art of Billingsgate
  I'll spare you, blushing reader).
'Whose is that shoddy little bus,
'Pathetic and ridiculous?
    'Without a doubt
    ' I'll sort him out,
  'The nasty little bleeder!'

'This *brutum fulmen* soon' he cried,
  (Quoting the Elder Pliny),
'Will vindicate my injured pride
'And push that puny car aside'
  'So grotty, cheap and tinny!
'We'll see' he said ' who calls the tune',
  And, edging up his huge saloon
    He spied ahead
    A flower bed,
And there he shoved the mini.

No guilt or feelings of remorse
  Disturbed this proud musician;
No thought that this high-handed course
Or arbitary use of force
  Should lead him to contrition.
The Cadillac, it stood to sense,
That symbol of his affluence,
   Furnished the might,
   And hence the right,
  That went with his position.

The concert hall came into view
  With neon lights that named him.
His fawning public never knew
The depths he had descended to,
  And therefore never blamed him.
So, having set aside his rage,
He arrogantly took the stage,
   And as he bowed
   The eager crowd
  Exultantly acclaimed him.

They started with a symphony
  (marked *poco animato*),
And soon an opportunity
To show his virtuosity
  Came with an *obbligato*.
In ecstasy he closed his eyes,
Re-opening them in surprise,
   And soon became,
   His cheeks aflame,
  As red as a tomato.

For as he played the solo part
  Like Heifetz or Grappelli,
Blissfully pouring out his heart
In unpremeditated art
  (To use a phrase of Shelley),

It was, alas, no shrill delight
That rent the fabric of the night -
    More of a groan
    Or undertone,
  Like rumblings in the belly.

He saw to his astonishment
  Among the double basses
An ardent soloist, intent
On grinding from his instrument
  (With suitable grimaces)
Whatever notes the leader played,
Repeated like a cannonade
    Three octaves low,
    Fortissimo,
  And louder still in places.

Back to his Cadillac once more
  His sobered way he wended.
There stood the mini. With a roar
It went, and from the driver's door
  Two fingers were extended.
'Remember, Mr Violin,
'The bigger one will always win;
    'So don't displace
    'A double bass!'
  And there the matter ended.

Pied Piper

One question always bugs me in
That stupid tale of Hamelin;
The piper lured the rats away,
But what the devil did he play?
The tiresome Browning never said,
And now regrettably he's dead.
To question him we're far too late;
All we can do is speculate.
A *Rondo*, we can safely say,
Would be a useless thing to play;
Having piped out his rodent train,
He'd find he'd piped them back again.
The River Weser, deep and wide,
We're told, lay on the southern side,
And when they reached the river bank,
They scampered in and promptly sank.
That was the way he dealt with them;
So what about a *Requiem*?
What should a piper choose to suit
His instrument?   'The Magic Flute'?
Or is the theme the crucial thing?
If so, a *Fugue* looks promising;
The Latin *fugo*, *fugere*,
Means 'scarper', 'do a bunk' or 'flee'.
The piper's son was said to play
'Over the hills and far away',
What seems more plausible to me
Is Haydn's Farewell Symphony.
The *Carnival des Animaux*
Looks possible at first, although
A loyal German rat would blench
At something so uniquely French;
Teutonic rats in Hamelin
Would sooner stomach *Lohengrin*!

Whatever theory we advance,
It's likely to have been a dance.
Some dances we can soon forget;
To rouse them with a minuet
Would be as hopeless as to try
And wake them with a lullaby.
I'm sure a foxtrot would be bound
To drive a rodent underground
A two-step wouldn't do instead,
Because a rat's a quadruped.
The hokey-cokey couldn't fail
To get them marshalled nose-to-tail,
And then, to get them moving quick,
A *Furiant* should do the trick!
What really happened who can tell?
But does it matter?   Does it hell?

55

Threnody for Saint Cecilia's Day

I'm Symphonic Sam
An' I come from West 'Am,
I'm ve man wiv ve musical nose.
Piu molto, piu poco
I play on my boko
Cadenzas and *harpeggios*.
I used to play Brahms
An' ve metrical psalms;
(Vey come over nice on ve snout),
But I can't get a squeak
From me perishin' beak
Since vey whistled me adenoids out.

I played an *Andante*
With Jimmy Durante
An' suffered a crushin' defeat;
Now from my piano
A bust of Cyrano
Leers down to remind me I'm beat.
An' ven wiv delight
I remember ve night
When I frilled all ve Festival 'All;
'Cos what a schimozzle
When I gits me schnozzle
Stuck into ve *Dead March in Saul*.

I didn't 'alf labour
At Schubert an' Weber;
It's no bleedin' work for a dunce.
In ve *Songs Wivout Words*
Vere's a passage in firds
Where you're 'ootin' bofe nostrils at once.
I can tone down me 'oots

If I bungs in me mutes,
But vey acts like a couple o' plugs,
An' Mozart's *Cassations*,
Squeezed fru me Eustachians,
Come whimpering aht o' me lugs.

I once played a trio -
Allegro con brio -
For schnozzle and double violin,
When a bloody great whistle
Comes aht o' me gristle
An' frightens me aht o' me skin.
In one competition
I met vis 'musician';
I'd not 'ave 'im collar ve cup!
So to git 'armonic
I blew somefink chronic
An' knackered me sinuses up.

Last night in a dream
I was lettin' orf steam
An' makin' a row like ve blitz ,
When I blew such an 'onk
On me perishin' konk
Vat I shattered ve bastard to bits;
An' I reads on vis stone,
Standin' vere all alone
Watchin' over my final repose:
'Ere lies Symphonic Sam
As came from West 'Am
An' died of a musical nose!'

Moments Musicaux

I
The music of Benjamin Britten
Was always impeccably written
  To appeal to the ears
  Of the late Peter Pears,
But I can't say I'm terribly smitten.

II
The sopranos in Handel's *Messiah*
Are required to sing hiah and hiah,
  Which is why more and more
  Get fed up with the score,
And use it for lighting the fiah.

III

The Victorians used to adore
The musical prowess of Spohr;
  But the pundits today
  In their high-handed way
Have written him off as a bore.

IV

The Englishman, William Boyce,
Had a rather peculiar voice;
  When people enquired
  Whom he chiefly admired,
He'd say 'Purcell is awfully noice.'

V

Young Mendelssohn's art was supreme
When he wrote his *Midsummer Night's Dream*.
  He was still going great
  When, at age thirty-eight,
He suddenly ran out of steam.

VI

Said Chopin, 'I cannot think what
'This gloomy old monastery's got;
  'But an evening *sub rosa*
  'Can make Valdemosa
'A rather agreeable spot.'

VII

That eccentric Hungarian, Liszt,
Exclaimed 'If you really insiszt
  'That the Danube is blue
  'It can only mean yue
'Must be quite unbelievably piszt!'

VIII
Said Schubert 'I haven't a doubt
'My symphony's not working out;
  'If I ever complete it
  'I still couldn't eat it,
'So why don't I stick to the Trout?

IX
The organist, Dr John Blow,
Was an obstinate character, so
  When the King asked him, 'Can ya
  'Compose *Rule Britannia?*'
He answered decisively, 'No!'

X
Said Bach, 'I don't get in a flap
'When they tell me my music is crap,
  ''Cos between you and me
  'I'm inclined to agree;
'I'm a pretty well-tempered old chap.'

XI
The image of poor old Scarlatti
Is starting to look rather tatty.
  His keyboard technique
  Is undoubtedly *chic*,
But it's driving the neighbourhood scatty.

XII
'I must have some money!', said Suk
'And I haven't a clue where to luk,
  'But I'll wed Dvorak's daughter
  'And that way I aughter
'Be able to get off the huk.'

XIII
That irascible character, Tallis,
Displayed his habitual malice,
  When the king put a ban on
  His new fangled cannon,
By firing his balls at the palace.

XIV
Rossini was thought rather odd -
A not-really-with-it old sod.
  When he sat in his arbour
  Composing *The Barber*,
He headed the score 'Sweeney Todd'.

XV
Frau Mozart was never a beauty,
But her voice was seductively fruity.
  When she lured him to bed
  It was then that he said
(In Italian) 'Cosi Fan Tutte!'

XVI
The catholic, William Byrd,
Played a seventh instead of a third.
  Said one music critic
  'The man's paralytic!
'He ought to be seen and not heard!'

XVII
That honest old Frenchman, Ravel,
Confided 'My vision of Hell
  'Is that ghastly *Bolero*!
  'I'd give it a zero,
'And shoot the composer as well!'

63

V. Sport

Match of the Day

Come, gentle Muse, and with athletick Fire
Kindle the Fancy, and the Pen inspire
To laud their Anticks and their Deeds extol
Who now assault, and now defend, the Goal!
Resplendent Beacons in th'advancing Night
From lofty Turrets pour contrived Light
On lustrous Lines, in long Dimension drawn
To trace the Margins of the verdant Lawn.
The alien Warriors first, to scornfull Dirge,
From subterraneous Catacombs emerge,
As when Persephone, from Stygian Night,
Arose, expectant, in th'unwonted Light;
And, all regardless of th'impending Fall,
Th'unwitting Victims dally with the Ball.
Nor merry Pan, nor Orpheus with his Lute
Made Strains more sweet than those which now salute
The Crew who sable Breeches interpose
'Twixt amber Tunicle and amber Hose.
The Clarion sounds, and soon from End to End
In ritual Strife th'opposing Ranks contend;
Ecstatic Swains in rude, discordant Style
Acclaim the skilfull and the Rest revile.
Mark how yon Forward, furious in Attack,
By devious Paths outstrips the slothfull Back;
With hidden Cunning and with Craft conceal'd
He gains the further Margin of the Field,
In humbler Mood the ancient Saw to rue:
'They nothing gain who to Excess pursue!'
But soon the Striker, with approving Nod,
Marking the Orb, which, from the distant Sod,
His stalwart Captain drove with measur'd Might,
Deflects it from its predetermin'd Flight
With fleet Deception and Composure cool

65

To lodge it in the pendent Reticule!
Ye righteous Gods! Ye Guardians of the Law!
And ye who blindfold Justice hold in Awe!
Assist yon Courier, who, in headlong Course,
Stumbles, impeded by unlawfull Force!
Grant Vengeance swift! Let well-directed Shot
Exact the Forfeit from th'appointed Spot!
But if to few the Marksman's Laurels go,
It falls to many to repulse the Foe.
Let all unite, in steadfast Purpose met,
To guard inviolate the virgin Net,
Whose scarlet-mantled Keeper, leaping high,
Snatches th'inflated Bladder from the Sky,
Or scorns the Missile of th'opposing Host
And, prostrate plunging, steers it round the Post.
And, lest the Tide of Battle bear away
Some luckless Corse untimely from the Fray,
Or falt'ring Footsteps earn condign Disgrace
For artless Knaves, in yon sequester'd Place
Sits one accoutred to receive the Call:
Sweet Consolation for a Comrade's Fall!
Now weari'd Thews and listless Limbs rejoice
To hear the strident Whistle's latest Voice;
Unlicens'd Infants trespass on the Sward
Where each pays Homage to his favour'd Lord.
As savage Swains depart in wild Array
With jocund Gesture and with ribald Lay,
Descends once more the sable Shroud of Night
To shade the martial Field from mortal Sight.
Farewell, thou trampled Turf, whose earthen Soul
Lies bar'd before the Face of either Goal!
Ye refuse-burthen'd Terraces, farewell,
Whose voided Flagons tawdry Tidings tell!
Farewell, ye Warriors, who the Sword transmute
If not to Ploughshare, then to nimble Boot!
Farewell, who win the Day, farewell who lose,
And fare thee well, O patient, gentle Muse.

The Spondulics: A Sonnet

Athletics is the highest form of art:
Motion and grace forged into poetry.
It sets the human enterprise apart
And clothes it with a magic quality.
This noble and enduring mystery,
Which sublimates and civilises strife,
Lifts the coarse passions of humanity
Above the trivialities of life.
Bring out the laurels!   Have the flags unfurled!
What other triumph of the human mind
Can so transcend the base, material world
By effort, skill and elegance combined?
These are the qualities I have to thank
For all that lovely lolly in the bank.

Struwwelpeter in Wimbeldheim

(With acknowledgments to Dr Heinrich Hoffmann)

When Johnny marches out on court,
He has his own idea of sport;
His only thought is how to win;
See what a state he's getting in!
For when the umpire had the nerve
To disallow a winning serve,
He screamed and waved his arms about,
Protesting 'That was never out!
Not within half a mile of it,
You fat, myopic, four-eyed git!'
The umpire, looking rather grave,
Exclaimed 'Oh Johnny, *please* behave!'
The tears ran down his cheeks so fast,
They made a little pond at last.
But Johnny, showing no regret
Nor any sense of etiquette,
Reviled the umpire clear and loud

Infuriating all the crowd,
Who shook their fists at him and cried
'He ought to be disqualified!'
But little Johnny didn't care;
And flung his racquet in the air.
He swore at everyone around;
And in his rage he beat the ground;
He beat the air, he beat the net;
He even beat an usherette;
And oh! far worse than all beside'
He beat the line-judge till she cried.

All the people round about
Waved their arms and shouted out
'Look at Little Johnny there,
Little Johnny Curse-'n-Swear!'

One evening on the Centre Court
 A figure of a different sort
Was sitting in the umpire's chair -
The great Agrippa, tall and spare.
He called out in an angry tone
'Boy, leave that naughtiness alone!'
But, ah! he did not mind a bit
What great Agrippa said of it;
He went on ranting as before,
And howled and roared and screamed and swore.
See the naughty, restless child
Growing still more rude and wild!
Then great Agrippa foamed with rage;
Look at him on this very page!

He clapped his hands; and in he ran
The great, long, red-legged racquet-man,

Who picked up Johnny Curse-'n-Swear
And banged him high into the air.
Soon he got to such a height,
He was nearly out of sight.
See him now, a tiny speck
Above the roofs of Tooting Bec.
No one ever yet could tell
Where he stopped, or where he fell:
Only this one thing is plain,
He was never seen again!

The Anabolics (or Hypodermics)

A toast to sport and sportsmanship! Play up and play the game!
And never be distracted by an easy path to fame.
The gentlemanly values that for centuries prevailed
Have met unwonted pressures and pathetically failed.
We see the torch of fellowship no longer burning bright;
Only the likes of you and me can keep the flame alight.
That girl who broke her leg, for instance, caused me deep remorse;
(It happened when I tripped her up - by accident of course);
But when I sent a floral spray to ease my peace of mind
I'm bound to say her attitude was anything but kind.
Those are the sort of people one would really like to shoot.
They smear the name of sport and bring it into disrepute.
They've got no time for discipline; they seem to think that rules,
Like honour and integrity, are only meant for fools.
And as for common decency, they treat it with disdain;
No wonder sport and sportsmanship are going down the drain!
Some people, on the other hand, will take too strict a line,
And criticise an understanding attitude like mine.
One naturally must allow some flexibility,
Or nobody would ever win, and then where should we be?
So when I need to have jab, as now and then I do,
I never ask them what it's for; it's better not to know.
It could be for malaria or typhoid possibly,
Or something else innocuous like Hepatitis B.
A reasonable person wouldn't call it underhand,
To take a little pick-me-up unless you know it's banned.
Everyone's code of ethics has some microscopic gaps,
And aren't we all entitled to a momentary lapse?
Although I try to bend the rules as little as I can,
I've reached the women's final, though I am, in fact, a man.
Perhaps this did necissitate some teeny-weeny lies,

But if I pass the urine test I'll sure accept the prize.
So here's to sport and sportsmanship! Play up and play the
game!
And never be distracted by an easy path to fame.
We wouldn't sell our self-respect, but if we ever did,
There'd be some consolation in a hundred thousand quid!

The Tiresome Turf

The first of August is a date
  I'd rather not remember.
He met me at the Member's Gate,
  (He is, of course, a Member).
After a feeble peck or two
  And two or three embraces,
The swine found nothing else to do
  But watch the bleeding races!

I'd bought *the* most expensive hat -
  A fabulous invention -
But could I get the stupid prat
  To give it his attention?
When I am looking really *chic*
  He's on about 'the going',
Worse than those thugs in Henley Week
  Who go to watch the rowing!

Suppose *you'd* spent three hours or more
  In thoughtful preparation;
Wouldn't *you* then be looking for
  A word of admiration?
Why take me racing on the flat,
  Why take me steeplechasing,
When all the time he's gawping at
  The pox-infested racing?

If you'd spent fortunes on your hair,
  Wouldn't it be upsetting
To see the bastard standing there
  Just working out the betting?
And then in the refreshment tent,
  While waiting for our ices,

Without a murmur off he went
  To read the latest prices.

Now what the Jockey Club should do
  Is set about replacing
Its antiquated point of view
  And cut out all this racing.
The policy that has my vote
  For all my favourite courses
Is 'Sack the jockies, shut the Tote,
  And shoot the bloody horses!'

VI FOOD

If Garlic be the Food of Love

'If garlic be the food of love, move on'.

It's quite astonishing how some
Will eulogise the *allium*.
They'll argue that a clove or two
Works wonders for a wholesome stew.
They'll take a tasty cut of lamb
Or veal or venison or ham
Or any other kind of meat
And render it unfit to eat.
Yes, many a garlic devotee
Has championed its pungency.
As Shakespeare very nearly said,
'Anne hath a way with garlic bread!'
In love and culinary skill
The French have always topped the bill;
The paradox that puzzles me
Is how they can successfully
Combine the art of making love
With reverence for the fetid clove.
The prelude, so it seems to me,
To coital activity
Demands a spot of common sense
And weeks of garlic-abstinence;
For how can halitosis be
An aid to nuptial ecstasy?
Or is it simply that the French
Are unaffected by the stench,
Their sensitivities destroyed,
Their taste buds rendered null and void,
Reduced to incapacity
By alliaceous gluttony?
Whatever be the reason for

Its high repute, I'll have no more!
It's surely time to call its bluff
And bury this disgusting stuff.
The die-hard gourmets may protest
That garlic-poisoned food is best,
But my researches hitherto
Have led me to this point of view:
One whiff is quite enough to prove
That garlic's *not* the food of love.

Cautionary Tale

My Lady Mayoress views with approbation
The silver ciphers of an invitation.
Of all the duties of her civic station
None is more worthy in her estimation
Than gracing a municipal collation.
Treating her palate first to titillation
By the delights of Spanish fermentation,
The heroine of this our recitation
Initiates with evident elation
The juicy processes of mastication.
The niceties of cultured conversation
Give place to uninhibited gustation,
Whereby her thwarted civic aspiration,
Rising above a lifetime of frustration,
Achieves a most congenial sublimation
In nourishing her private corporation.
The moral of this dismal denigration,
Which is that alimentary inflation
Should subject be to rigid limitation,
Lies in its miserable culmination.
My Lady Mayoress, in anticipation
Of the more tiresome task of concentration
On My Lord Mayor's post-prandial oration,
Contemptuous of decent moderation,
Scoops up some sweet and sickly preparation
Known as a *mousse*, or some such appellation,
One spoonful past the point of satiation.
Bang goes her belt - and bang her reputation!

The Making of Apple Chutney

No cultured person will dispute
The apple is the king of fruit;
To pick and eat one from the tree
Is gastronomic ecstasy.

Though Holy Scripture does not state
What was the fruit that Adam ate,
Tradition says the apple is
The fateful fruit of Genesis.

My lady wife, God bless her heart,
Enjoys the culinary art;
She takes some apples in a bowl
And deftly peels them, bless her soul!

Ten minutes with the kitchen knife
Are ample for my lady wife,
And when she has them peeled and cored
She chops them on her chopping-board.

'Aha!   The scene is set!' say I;
'God send it be an apple pie
'To which my lady sets her hands!'
'Amen!' say my saliva glands.

My lady wife, I soon perceive,
Seems to be laughing up her sleeve;
And soon the fruity fragments are
Immersed in boiling vinegar.

But even that is not enough.
She shovels in all sorts of stuff:
Spices and onions, garlic too,

And leaves it on the stove to stew.

Recording Angel, take a look
And open up your record-book.
Such vandalistic acts demand
At least a gentle reprimand.

When Eve urged Adam on to sin,
Her indiscretion ended in
Their joint expulsion, but today
Adam alone is turned away.

For now the choking, acrid fumes
Have permeated all the rooms,
And till the air be purified
My own abode I can't abide.

So, leaning on my garden gate,
I stand and brood, disconsolate,
On apples, onions, kitchen knives,
And vinegar . . . and lady wives!

The Dietetics

I tell the tale of Rupert Gray,
  A fine upstanding figure,
A stalwart man in every way,
Big as a guardsman, I should say,
  And arguably bigger.
People considered him to be
A model of sobriety,
    Dignified, proud,
    And well-endowed
  With energy and vigour.

His Aunt Matilda came to pay
  An unexpected visit,
But when she saw the breakfast tray
It made her turn an ashen grey
  And gasp 'Whatever is it?
'Bacon and egg, dear boy?   It's fried!
'The worst thing you could have!' she cried,
    'We can't eat that!
    'Animal fat
'Is totally illicit!'

For lunch a juicy T-bone steak
  He thought would be delicious.
His visitor was quick to take
Exception to this grave mistake;
  She called him meretricious.
'Red meat is lethal, don't you know?
'And *beef* particularly so;
    'This BSE
    'Is known to be
  'Exceptionally vicious!'

'Twas then she started to impart
  A wealth of information
About the culinary art,
(The subject closest to her heart)
  And its degeneration,
And how the standard of *cuisine*
Is worse than it has ever been,
    And all the meat
    We have to eat
  Shows some contamination,

She worked on his credulity,
  (For such was her intention),
By painting scenes of misery
And unrelieved calamity
  Too numerous to mention.
And as she rattled on apace
She noted that young Rupert's face
    To her delight
    Was turning white
  With growing apprehension.

'And what's for dinner, dear?' she said,
  Regarding him severely.
Rupert, now turning rather red,
Was thus obliged to scratch his head
  And rack his brains, for clearly
Red meat was permanently off;
(Forget about that *Stroganoff!*)
    Perhaps a bite
    Of something light
  Would fit the bill more nearly.

He cleared his throat: 'I've just the thing'
 He said, 'a chicken curry.'
'Chicken! You'll have us sickening
'From *salmonella* poisoning.
 'd sooner dine on slurry!
 r those of us who really care
 he signs are written everywhere;
   'It's only those
   'Who choose to close
 'Their eyes that need to worry!'

The harass'd Rupert thought of fish
 And found a tempting fillet.
'Now this would make a tasty dish;
'Not fried, of course, but if you wish,
 'I thought perhaps I'd grill it."
'Seafood' she cried 'is just obscene!
'Re-cycled effluent, you mean!
   'And grilling it
   'A little bit
 'Won't make it safer, will it?'

She pestered him for five more days
 Before her visit ended.
In subtle, cunning, devious ways
She fertilised his nascent craze
 Precisely as intended,
Persisting in her plan, till he
Was quite as paranoid as she,
   And when she thought
   She had him caught,
 Her homeward way she wended.

Though certain in her scheming mind
 That Rupert was converted,
She thought it best to leave behind
Some useful books for him to find
 With little notes inserted

On sugars, fats and alcohol,
And caffeine and cholesterol,
  And heart disease,
  And things like these,
For fear that he reverted.

So Aunt Matilda's little plot
  Turned out to be a winner.
Rupert, contented with his lot,
At first found dishes, which were not
  Injurious, for dinner;
But one by one he struck them out,
As some incriminating doubt
  Entered his mind,
  And soon we find
He started growing thinner.

Disquieting discoveries
  Reduced the menu quickly.
He found that bread has calories
And that bacteria in cheese
  Can kill if spread too thickly.
Unprocess'd bran was safe enough,
And, though he couldn't stand the stuff,
  He packed away
  A pound a day
And found it pretty prickly.

The drastic steps he chose to take
  Cut down his weight severely.
No compromises would he make;
Nothing could cause him to forsake
  Principles held sincerely;
And when our dietetic friend
Met his inevitable end,
  In language terse
  This little verse
Summ'd up the story clearly:

85

'Remember, ye who pass this way,
  'That human life is fleeting.
'Mark well the fate of Rupert Gray;
'For him celestial trumpets bray
  'And heavenly drums are beating,
'Who, from the day he saw the light,
'Renounced temptation day and night.
    'A frugal man,
    'He lived on bran
  'And died of healthy eating.'